JOE TANNER

NOT THINKING STRAIGHT

Answers for the straight person's questions from a gay man

First edition

This book was professionally typeset on Reedsy.
Find out more at reedsy.com

I dedicate this book to my mom. She passed away in January 2019. She was my best friend. I miss her with all of my gay heart! Thank you, mom, for loving me, no matter what. Thank you for showing me unconditional love when I needed it most. Thank you to my siblings who have been such a great support and source of joy for me in my hard times. I love you all with "all of my heart, might, mind and strength."

Contents

Preface

Hi! I'm Joe! I wrote this book because I wanted to provide a resource to all the straight people in the world who are curious about the LGBTQIA+ community. I listed a bunch of questions I have personally been asked by straight people during my journey, as well as statements I have heard from religious groups. My hope is that I will create more understanding and bridge some gaps in people's understanding. I also hope that it will help gaybies (gay babies–not literal babies, but those brand new to being gay) to step into their power and understand that the way they feel is okay. It is natural. I hope it helps them in their journey along their way. I also hope it helps parents of gay kids, who are trying to navigate their way through having an LGBTQIA+ person in their family, when they weren't necessarily expecting it.

1

Why did you choose to be gay?

Have you ever been in a situation where you felt like you were having an out of body experience—while you were having a conversation with someone? I feel like this happens to me a fair amount. Almost like I am watching a movie play out about my life and this conversation I am having with another person, only I am watching it play out because it doesn't feel like it can be real. Like I am in an episode of "the Wonder Years" and feel as though someone else is narrating what is happening in my life.

It's those moments when someone asks you a question that makes you feel so out of your element, or makes you feel small or helpless, and until you have had a chance to think about it and process how you would better respond. You sit there dumbfounded and feeling like an idiot. Feeling like you don't even know yourself.

There have been so many times that someone asked me a question, and I didn't know how to respond—either because I genuinely didn't know the answer, I couldn't believe they were asking me the question, or I was worried more about hurting the other person's feelings or crushing their beliefs, through my answers.

I grew up a very faithful and devout Mormon. ***if you are worried you won't understand ANY of this, because of that–I promise you still will. I only share that for context of who I was and to point out that I was very religious*** There were so many things that I never allowed myself to question, think about, or believe. To quote The Book of Mormon Musical, "Mormons just believe."

I lived in a world where my beliefs of what was true, were ingrained in me from the time I was a "Sunbeam" (which is what they call children in a primary/learning course on Sundays that consists of mainly 4 and 5-year-old children) because "Jesus wanted me to shine for Him each day."

By the time I got into Junior High and High School, I thought *for sure* I had met at least 10,000 people in my life, and 99% of them were all Mormon. So, naturally, Mormonism was the right and correct religion—because my parents and leaders would *never* lie to me, and they *knew* what was right, because they had more life experience. Forget the fact that they lied to me about Santa, the Easter Bunny, and the Tooth Fairy. I'm sure they lied to me about hundreds of things—all well intentioned—but still a lie.

It became so easy to just follow along and do whatever I was told. Mormonism, teaches that obedience is the first law of heaven—do what you are told. Follow the Prophet. Listen to your parents and church leaders. Trust them. You don't know any better. You are too young (but not too young to choose to be *baptized* and *join* the faith at 8 years old).

I believe that obedience is helpful to teach kids—as long as you give them a *why* behind what you are asking them to do. We obey laws so that we can stay safe. We put on seat belts, and buy insurance, and don't speed (or shouldn't)—so we can stay SAFE.

But what happens when the "laws" that you are taught to follow and believe don't keep you safe and actually cause a lot of self-harm, depression, anxiety, and sadness? Do those sound like laws you would want to follow? I don't believe you would—in your right mind. However, when you are kept in a bubble, and you associate everything that is "safe" to church, you are more likely to act in the way you are told. You are told over and over that your safety, peace, and happiness ALL come from going to church and listening to "the Prophet and His Apostles." It makes it really hard to venture out into a "very dangerous" world. A world that would supposedly make you even more sad than what you already are feeling from staying in the "safety" of that church.

I grew up knowing that I liked boys (when I was a boy—men, now that I am a man) from the time I was 6 years old. However, I also learned *very early* that I wasn't *supposed* to like boys, and that it was *very wrong*, because that is what I was taught. So, I practiced, watched, listened, and observed other boys, and men to try and figure out what made them so different from me. I did everything I could to try and blend in.

I had so many conversations with friends about how hot I thought a girl was, and I always would choose one that was clearly a favorite of all of the straight guys, while secretly being in love with the boys at my school and hating myself for it. I still found out ways to be happy and tried to focus on those, because I couldn't have anyone thinking that something was wrong with me—most of all God, who was ultimately going to take my gayness away from me, because I was praying so hard for it, and "God hears and answers our prayers."

Don't get me wrong, I believe that our prayers are answered, but not in the way we always think or believe. My prayers finally got answered when I allowed myself to be more real and authentic. They were answered when I allowed myself to ask questions that I never let myself ask before. My prayers were answered when I realized that I deserved to have true happiness, and follow my heart and my truth–I just had to learn to love myself, and others, differently.

When I finally came out the second time—the real time (more about that later), I was surprised when someone asked me "what made you choose to be gay?" I was taken back. I jumped out of my body, and felt like it was hours before I responded, when in actuality it was probably only a few seconds. I felt paralyzed. Did I *choose* to be gay? Absolutely not.

To me, that question was sort of like asking a tree (if it could respond) when did you choose to be a Pine tree? I don't think it would respond "well, I realized I didn't have any leaves like the other trees, so I decided I couldn't be a regular tree anymore, I had to be a Pinetree—probably because I have needles, and smell like pine, and have Pinecones, so I decided to be Pine. But that doesn't make me less than the other trees. I still have value as a tree." That tree was created that way. It didn't have to choose or explain anything about its existence, it just did what it was born to do.

So why did I respond the way I did? My response was something to the effect of "I just couldn't live a lie anymore." Now, most people would argue that that is a great response. There is nothing wrong with it. I *shouldn't* have to lie—and they would be right. However, I don't think it actually answers the question. I didn't *choose* to be gay. I always WAS gay; I just chose not to tell anyone so that I could fit in. I didn't understand the difference between fitting in and belonging.

The way that I wish I would have responded in that moment, and the way I respond to that question now, is: "When did you choose to be straight?

Choice implies that you are given options to select from, so tell me when you were ever presented with the option(s),
    do you:
    a) want to be straight?
    b) want to be gay (or any other form of LGBTQIA+)?

In today's world, even though there is more acceptance of those who are different, we have a LONG way to go. Who would *choose* to be something that many people seem to hate or treat poorly? Who would *choose* to be someone who doesn't have equal rights in the world? Why would someone *choose* to be a person who is viewed as going to hell–for something they didn't actually *choose* to **feel** and **be**?"

Most people tend to choose the path of least resistance. So why don't we applaud those who are different from us? The ones who are different are the ones who open our eyes, minds, and hearts to things that bring more beauty and joy into our lives. Afterall, variety is the spice of life, right? So let us all be our own "trees" so that we can add variety and diversity into our lives.

If you believe that God created the world, then you must also believe that God is the author of diversity in everything that was created. Look at all of the different forms of trees, plants, flowers, mountains, valleys, deserts, shrubs, landscapes, animals, oceans, lakes, rivers, etc, that all are different and serve a purpose of some kind. All of these different things help you to appreciate the things that we sometimes take for granted.

Why would God stop in creating things with a purpose when it comes to human beings? Clearly we all look, think, act, and feel different about so many things. You would be hard-pressed to find anyone who hasn't been challenged by something or someone that they didn't know before—when they are open and willing to learn from them.

Just because gay people can't procreate, doesn't mean that God doesn't love them. Afterall, if that was the case, why did God create animals and plants that don't need another gender to create life? Maybe we just need to redefine what it means to create a life and live a life—with love and purpose.

You know what the great thing is about most Christians? They usually believe in forgiveness. So, I am asking all Christians, to forgive themselves for treating their LGBTQIA+ brothers and sisters so poorly, both now, and in the past—so that we can both move forward together as people. As Humans. Humans who love and help each other to get our needs met. Humans that meet and fulfill their purpose and their destiny.

2

Have you tried NOT being gay?

When you were young, did your mom ever say anything like "if all of your friends jumped off a cliff, would you do it too?" yeah, mine did as well. If yours didn't, you probably never got in trouble, or wanted to do something that you just felt like you *had* to do, or you would die!

Here is the funny thing. If all my friends were gay, I *could* have been myself. I *would* have been *completely* happy jumping off that gay cliff!!! However, none of my friends were actually gay (that I knew of anyway), so instead, I had to try NOT to be gay–Every. Single. Day. Of. My. Life. Until I was in my early thirties.

I was jumping off a proverbial straight cliff, but I should have really taken my mother's advice and NOT done what all the boys around me were doing—liking girls, dating girls...or having sex with them (not having sex with them was easy for me, so I can't say I actually jumped off THAT cliff).

What kinds of things did this proverbial straight cliff teach me? It taught me that it was ok to hurt girls and lead them on (news flash, it is NOT!). It taught me that it is more important to fit in, than to be myself and *belong*. It taught me that being fake will help you win friends and influence people—but not in a real or meaningful way.

With all of the questions that have been asked—which helped me to write this book, I want to always flip them for the straight people of this world and ask "Have you tried NOT being straight?" Because as stated before, you didn't choose to be straight. So asking someone to completely change their attractions is a tall order. But honestly, if you tried NOT being straight, you *might actually* like it. ☺ No? Mmmmm K. Don't ask the gays to do what you aren't willing to do yourself. I'm pretty sure that should be in the 10 commandments or something.

If you are a good-looking straight guy who is willing to take this advice—I volunteer as tribute for your first gay experience. I promise to be gentle and make it worth your while. It might be kind of like when brunets try to go blonde—because "blondes have more fun." Don't knock it until you try it.

So many people seem to be fine accepting Gluten, but not Gay. Why is that? Isn't gluten God's creation? Some people's bodies are just built differently and need something different to feel happy and healthy. God's creations are full of variety for a reason.

I understand people wanting to ask this question of, "have you tried NOT being gay," when they have been raised and taught to believe that everyone must be the same (even though they clearly do not).

Some examples of things that we would be missing out on if that variety didn't exist:

- What if James Bond never starred Daniel Craig, because he just didn't "look the part" according to traditional Bonds–and he is my FAVORITE Bond Character.
- If Taylor Swift always stayed country because "that is who she is" or "Country Music is God's Music," then we would have never had 1989, Reputation, Lover, Evermore, and Folklore, Midnights, and now TTPD!!! That woman is a Goddess!!!
- What if Beyonce never went country?!?! Cowboy Carter is a masterpiece. That woman can really do anything she wants. She is also a Goddess!!!
- What if Whitney Houston just stayed in modeling???
- If Garth Brooks wasn't the wavemaker that he was (look it up— people were banning him from their homes and radio stations because of "The Thunder Rolls" and "We shall be free.") we would never have got to experience those amazing songs along with many others like "If tomorrow never comes" and "Ain't Goin' Down" and MANY more.
- Cheesecake—think about it. If there was ONLY NY Style Cheese-cake. It would be a SHAME!!!
- Wines, beers, and sodas. There are days that I would CUT someone to get a Dr. Pepper. (not really, I don't condone violence, but I had to make a point that Dr Pepper is the nectar of the Gods–especially when you add coconut creamer to it...YUM).

My point is, variety is the spice of life. Diversity exists in so many forms and it exists that way for a reason. If something isn't hurting you or hurting other people, then why are we making such a big deal out of it? If you are a religious person, why are you so worried about MY salvation, when you really should be worrying about your own? If we are commanded to love one another and the love that you are "showing" to others is making them hate themselves or not want to live anymore, then you probably need to discover a different kind of love.

3

Does God love a gay?

The idea of God is beautiful—when you take away all of the "vengeful" this and "mighty wrath" that. I have a hard time believing that a God would be so mean, vengeful, and full of wrath—especially as an evolved being who knows all and sees all. Why would he (or she, or they) get mad and angry at us, when we are just down here trying to figure our shit out?!

Frustrated? Sure. Angry? Probably. Vengeful? **Absolutely not.** If you are a parent, I know you have been frustrated or angry with your kids at some point, but when have you actually thought you are going to exact your revenge on them because they didn't listen to you, or do exactly what you told them? My guess is you wouldn't do that–and if you would, you should probably see a therapist and get some help. If you can love your kids and forgive them, when you yourself are not perfect or evolved, then why couldn't God?

How many of you grew up in an abusive home? Even if you were straight? How many of you promised yourself you wouldn't be like your abuser? Why would you promise yourself that? I'll tell you why—

it's because you know it isn't the way. You know it isn't healthy. You know that it only gets people to do what you want out of fear—not love. So you promised to do better. But did you become perfect? No. You still made mistakes, and you know when and where you made them.

So—if God is a perfect being who has been around for eternity, why would he *still* be getting angry at us—who have only been here for xx amount of years (insert whatever age you are)?! I just don't believe that that is a thing.

We talk so much about God and Jesus as a nation, but we don't always act in the ways that we should. When we treat another human poorly—even though "Jesus said love everyone," we are not acting in our highest good. Our accountability doesn't change (or shouldn't—but sometimes attorneys have a way of changing that) when we say "but so and so told me to do it." You still have your agency in the matter.

Sometimes, it can feel as though the straight people who don't understand gay people (aka—bigoted people) go on these missions to tear down, belittle, bully, or to harass gay people—who are just trying to live their lives in peace, all under the guise of "but God told me to do it."

When did Jesus *ever* say, "thou shalt hate the gays," Or "gay people are a sin?" Show me in the bible where it says that? You can't—because it doesn't exist. And even if it did (which it doesn't), is your church holding straight people to the same standards when they sin? I would argue that they aren't.

MEN are creating the thought and teaching that "it's not natural," or "it's an abomination in the sight of God." If we are going off things that are not natural, let's talk about plastic, Hostess Twinkies, people flying through the air in a giant piece of metal, or how about plastic surgeries??? But are those all okay because they serve the purpose of men?

Maybe straight men and women who fear gay people just need to be more aware of how gay people serve a purpose.

I believe God *loves* the gays because He created us. He created Gays so that they could help straight men not be so dumb with their wives and girlfriends. He created Gays to help beautify the world. He created gays to help balance out the toxic masculinity that exists. He created Gays to give straight women hope that there are still good and kind men out there. He created Gays so that Queer Eye and Ru Paul could exist.

4

Is God a Man or a Woman? Does it even matter?

Straight men seem to worship women, so why couldn't a woman be a God? They tend to do things for women that they would never do for anyone else. It is a deeper kind of worship. They worship their bodies, and they worship what a woman offers them. They also worship athletes, but Athletes don't have the same power and control over them. Perhaps it is because they don't have a sense of ownership and loyalty to the athlete.

I have seen multiple straight men idolize an athlete—until they disagree with something the athlete does or says. Once they lose respect for a difference of opinion, they write the athlete off. With a woman, though—it is different. A woman can disagree, persuade, and get a man to change his mind. But it is done so subtly, that the man doesn't even know it. An idol can only have power if we worship it.

I sometimes wonder if we truly believe what we say when we say we believe in God. If a God is omniscient and omnipotent, why would they be concerned with trivial matters? We act as if God only expresses sympathy and judgment. If God was truly what we say (s)he is, then I believe that God would be an empathetic God. One who sees our suffering, and mourns with us, and cries with us. God would be a deity that forgives quickly because they would understand our circumstances. They would understand our minds and hearts in the moments when we are not being our best selves and would take time to not only be with us but also show us a way forward and a way out of our messes.

Instead, people tend to worship a "God" that is the complete opposite of that. If we have truly learned to love ourselves and other people, we would allow them grace and space to make mistakes and be themselves. We would allow them to learn because even when learning is hard it still teaches us and shapes us to become better than we once were.

5

Why do you have to be in your underwear and parade around?

How many of us experience body shame? On some level, I believe we all do. There are things that every person doesn't like about their body. Even those with a "perfect" body sometimes end up resenting what that body represents. When someone is looked at as if the only thing they have that brings any value is their body, they tend to hate what others worship about them.

Have you ever wished that you could just be free? That you didn't have to worry about what other people were thinking about your body? Have you ever wished that you had enough confidence to wear that bathing suit you always wanted to wear? That you didn't have to cover up the parts of your body that make you insecure?

Someone being in their underwear, is expressing a type of freedom that most people want. It is saying that you don't have to conform to what everyone in society thinks or has been taught.

Nudists exist. Straight ones. All types of nudists. They live their life in a way that they try not to be confined or restricted by the things that they wear. Of course, there are rules and laws that exist for public nudity, but there are times and places. That is why bath-houses exist, and nude beaches.

Being in your underwear is the closest thing to that level of freedom— but it keeps things covered and still leaves *something* to the imagination. It isn't much different than going to the beach and seeing people in bikinis and speedos–but people tend to make a big deal out of it because it isn't something *they* would do. Why aren't they freaking out about what their kids see at the beach? It's not much different.

That is why hundreds of thousands of straight boys wank off to swimwear magazines. And those aren't being boycotted. Neither are the underwear ads that come to people's homes (which also get used by young men to pleasure themselves) in order to make money.

Should we go out and boycott any sort of advertisements about underwear? I don't know the answer, but I would venture to guess that if you asked any straight man if they *ever* perved out over those magazines and advertisements, I bet they all have. And they still turned out "normal" by societal standards.

In the end, I believe the purpose of LGBTQIA people being in their underwear at a parade is to let go of shame. Shame around our bodies, shame around the way we feel, shame around what society has deemed as "bad." It is a statement of saying, "Look at me in my most (or very close to) vulnerable state, and I refuse to be ashamed and embarrassed by it.

It is as natural as my sexuality, and my sexuality is something to be proud of—not hidden, covered up, or closeted.

6

How can it be natural if you can't procreate?

This is always such a funny argument to me. Can a rock procreate? Is it, then, not natural? Does that mean that every straight couple that is unable to have kids is also unnatural? No matter how hard they try, no matter how much science is trying to help, there are couples who never will have a chance to have children unless they adopt.

It also doesn't seem natural that Tom Cruise has to run in his movies as much as he does. I'm pretty sure that if you took a clip of just him running, from every movie he has ever made, you could make a full-length feature of his runs, alone.

When we use the word "natural," that word stems from nature. If you look at nature, there are hundreds of examples of plants and animals that do not need an opposite-gendered partner to procreate.

What you are really saying is—it isn't natural—to you. That is fine. We are not *asking* you to be gay or lesbian. We are not *asking* you to change your natural preferences.

Have you ever asked yourself if the fear and disgust that you have surrounding issues related to LGBTQIA things could just be some deep-seated envy that hasn't been healthily processed? Maybe you wish you could have the freedom to live authentic to how you feel, but you were taught or raised to believe that it was wrong, and if you can't live that way, then no one else should be able to?

If that is your line of thinking, then how is it different from a priest telling you that they have forsaken sex and marriage to be married to God, and so everyone else should have to do the same? Would you be willing to concede to that? Of course, you wouldn't.

Or what if your favorite alpha male decided to make a change in their life based on something that they loved, would the proverbial message from your mother of "if all your friends jumped off a cliff, would you do it too?" enter your mind?

What if your idol said they were going to swear off women and sports and drinking to become a dog trainer—because that is what brought them joy, would you do the same thing? I'm going to place my bets that you probably would not—unless you are obsessed with dogs—then maybe...but is that obsession with an animal "natural?" We may never know. Speaking of animals...this next chapter is all about them.

7

You don't see animals exhibit homosexual acts in nature, so it isn't natural.

his is simply not true. Did you know Dolphins regularly engage in "swordplay"? It is exactly what it sounds like. Remember when you and your brothers or friends would have "sword fights" with your urine streams? Well, this takes it a step further. Male dolphins often engage in "sword fights" with their erect penises—not their urine. Some never pair off with a female dolphin.

You will find plenty of examples of homosexual behavior in Bison, Penguins, Lions, white-tail deer, flamingos, gorillas, and the list goes on. Google it.

We look to nature for so many things—when it is convenient and when it supports our narrative. In a world filled with diversity, a world filled with so much variety, with organisms that are so complex and multifaceted, why wouldn't there be examples of homosexuality? Of course, there are—because it isn't wrong. It is simply different.

There are a lot of things that I could use in nature to fit a narrative if I wanted to. Animals hunt other animals down and kill them for food. Does that mean we should be killing other humans for food? Animals have sex with multiple partners; does that mean humans should too (not that there's anything wrong with that–just pointing that out for all the pro-marriage people)?

Animals go around in herds, whether they are family or not. Some hibernate, some don't. Some are vegetarian, some aren't. Some species the female is dominant, others it's the male. I could go on and on.

My point is—nature is a great example to look to for SO many things, AND we aren't animals. We have the right and ability to choose how we behave and treat others. We have the ability to cognitively think and reason. We are meant to evolve and not stay living in a past way of life that made people live in fear and hate.

8

Can't you just be celibate? It's what God would want

Would you want to be celibate? Would you want your kids to be celibate? Most humans crave touch, connectedness, and closeness. Most of us want to bond and feel a part of something greater than ourselves.

If God wanted anyone to be celibate, why did God create sex in the first place? Like—if it wasn't needed, if it wasn't meant to connect us on a different level, why does it exist?

If you argue that it is only for procreation, then why do straight couples still have sex without trying to make babies? If it is only for procreation, then why are there examples in nature that don't need/require a partner to procreate? If it is only for procreation, then why are there couples who CAN'T have children?

Also, if sex was ONLY meant for procreation, then why did the creator put an erogenous zone in the ass?

This really isn't an option for most people. If you honestly think that you could do it–why haven't you? Why would you wish or want that for another human?

9

I'm fine with gay people, but Trans people…

Have you ever not liked something about your body that you wish you could change? Maybe you would get liposuction, a tummy tuck, breast implants, hair plugs, lasik, laser hair removal, botox, face lift, calf implants, butt implants, breast reduction, braces, teeth whitening, etc. etc. etc.

When people make the argument that trans people aren't natural or aren't what God intended, I have to laugh…mostly because I don't want to be angry at them for their hypocrisy. All those things listed above are things that we have accepted as a society as totally fine—even though they aren't "natural" and aren't "the way God made you." Help me understand how any of that is different from receiving any form of gender-affirming care.

With how complex genetics and DNA are, it is no wonder that we have people who don't feel right in their bodies. I have two nephews who were born with actual breast tissue. The amount of stress that caused them and the effect it had on their confidence weighed heavy on them. They were teased and made fun of for it.

When they were old enough, they got surgery to remove their breast tissue. No one got upset about that. But if we go back to the thought, "that is not how God created you," then they could have never had that surgery. It did SO much to actually build their confidence and self-esteem. I was 100% in support of them getting it. I feel like most people who have any sort of empathy would also feel that way.

So—why is it bad for other children to not feel comfortable in their bodies? Why couldn't they receive hormone blockers (which are reversible), therapy, haircuts, and different kinds of clothes that make them feel more comfortable in their own skin?

Many conservative people seem to think that full sex change operations are taking place on these kids and seem to think that they will have regrets later in life about it. I have yet to find a trans person who has regretted going through a full gender assignment surgery. There may be those outliers, but that is why rules and regulations are in place for therapy (which is *required* for them to go through) and other steps that have to happen before they can go through with it.

For those of you who say that it is grooming our children: I want you to think of all of the socially acceptable ways that our children are currently being "groomed," and no one is batting an eye at them:

1. Girls who dance (even the very young ones) wear tiny/skimpy leotards and dresses and dance in VERY provocative ways. Some are even stuffing their costumes to make it look like they have breasts...at *twelve* years old.
2. Cheerleaders are putting their legs, midriffs, and breasts on display with very tiny cheerleading costumes.
3. Families take their little boys and girls to Hooters and have their

kids take pictures with the waitresses.

4. Families take their kids to the beach, where there are hundreds of men and women in speedos and bikinis.
5. Playing with GI Joe's or Barbie's as kids.
6. Teaching boys that it is not okay to cry or show emotion.
7. Beauty pageants
8. Sports that only men can play
9. Making girls play with baby dolls and dress up
10. Princesses and Princes.

I LOVE dance, it is one of my favorite expressions of art. I love cheerleaders, they make games for fun and engaging. I don't care for Hooters—but give me a male version of this, and YES, I am there. I love going to the beach. Those things did not make me be one way or another.

I can also argue that if seeing something makes you something, then **I would have 100% turned out straight.** Everything in my life that I grew up around modeled a very straight world. I didn't have any examples of anything gay in my life. All of the movies, books, television, and people were all very straight—and somehow, I was still able to find my gay self as an adult. Even when I *knew* I was attracted to men from the time I was six years old. I just thought everyone was and that they would just grow out of it or that it changed over time. It doesn't. I didn't.

I would invite you to challenge your way of thinking. Add a dash of humanity to your list of things that you want/need to work on in your imperfect state. Choose to show and demonstrate kindness–even when you don't understand.

10

Does being gay make you a child molester?

No. No, it does NOT! I have asked you to expand your thinking in so many ways. The exception I would make would be when it comes to Pedophelia. *Everything* about that is **WRONG!!!** Taking another's agency is NEVER an option.

I hate when people automatically assume that because I am gay, it automatically makes me a pedophile. It falls NOWHERE under the LGBTQIA+ banner.

Are there LGBTQIA+ people who could also be Pedophiles? Of course—just like there are straight, religious, and non-religious people who are.

I want to point out the massive difference in the LGBTQIA+ community wanting to expand our rights and what it means to be a Pedophile. Pedophilia is 100% taking away the agency of a child. That child is not old enough to make consent choices. A Pedophile tries to influence and make a child afraid and feel shameful and that they cannot ask for help because it could hurt or damage their family. NOTHING about this is ok. Someone in the LGBTQIA+ community wanting to have the same rights to love and relationships is being done by two (or more if there are thrupples or open relationships) *consenting* ADULTS. Anyone involved is old enough to make up their minds and choose to participate or not.

Wanting to have rights is VERY different from taking away the rights and agency of a child.

11

Have you tried sex with a woman?

irst of all–ewe. No. I have not. Even though that is none of your business, I am willing to share that I was a Gold Star Gay–meaning that I never had sex with or married a woman. There were girls that I knew in High School and College who wanted to have sex with me. It was VERY easy for me to say no under the guise that we had to be "good."

Most straight men ask me this because they can't imagine not having sex with a woman. I also can't imagine having sex with a woman, so we are the same, but just different.

They tend to think that if I just tried having sex with a woman, it would change my mind. Let me ask that question back to you: If you (assuming you are a straight man) could have sex with a man, do you think it would change your orientation or be something you could enjoy? When I ask that question back to them, they almost always say, "absolutely not." So why would or should it be different for a gay person?

If you (as a straight man) can say that you *could* enjoy sex with a man, then maybe you are a little Bi, or higher up on the Kinsey scale. That is ok, too.

To all my Lesbian, Bi, and Straight friends–I am SO happy that you love the female body and enjoy it to its fullest extent–it is not for me–and that is OK by me. I LOVE that journey for you. Leave me ALL the (non-toxic) men.

12

Are you the boy/girl husband/wife?

P lease get out of the habit of asking this question. Clearly, I am a man. My pronouns are HE/HIM. Most of the men I've dated have also had those same pronouns. I understand why you would ask it; you are so used to *traditional* relationships.

In today's world, those *traditional* roles have evolved—even in straight relationships. I know plenty of straight couples where the woman is the primary breadwinner, and the husband stays home with the kids. It works for them. Sometimes, the husband cooks and cleans and the wife does the laundry and shopping. Sometimes, both partners work and bring home money, and they send their children to daycare and take turns doing the cooking and cleaning or tackle them all together.

It doesn't matter who pays or who makes the money or does the cleaning or cares for the kids. Those things get done one way or another.

I think this is why there are more and more people who are gender non-conforming. They don't want to be labeled or reduced to something that they do, defining who they are.

None of us are all ONE thing. If someone is a dad, they can also be a husband, a brother, an uncle, a son, a friend, a teacher, a social worker, a movie critic, a Packers fan, etc.

13

What happened to you to make you this way?

I t is so interesting when I get asked this question. I used to believe that all of the reasons I was gay were due to the things people associate with being gay:

1. I had an absent father
2. I had a present mother
3. I had lots of sisters
4. I was molested by a guy when I was young
5. I didn't play sports enough
6. I was exposed to pornography before I was ready

I assumed that all of those things "made" me gay. But the funny thing is—I liked boys from the time I was 5 (to the extent that you can at that age). That was my earliest memory. I wanted to kiss the boys in my neighborhood. My dad *quickly* let me know that it *wasn't* ok. I didn't know it was "wrong." I just felt that way. Then, once I started going through puberty, I did NOT think about girls; I only thought about guys. That never went away—no matter how much I prayed and served God and avoided all sins. No matter how much therapy I went to. No matter how much I tried dating girls. No matter if I went through conversion therapy. None of it worked. I was meant to love men.

It took me a while to realize that those things were correlations–not causations. I met a guy when I was going to this church-sponsored program for LGBTQ members. When he told me his story, it unraveled a lot of things for me. When he told me he came from a home with a traditional and loving mom and dad, where they had healthy relationships and support. He had 5 brothers. He never watched pornography. He played sports. He was never molested. He had ZERO sisters, and yet–4 of the 5 brothers were gay. There was only ONE straight boy in their family of 5 boys. My mind was blown. I figured something *had* to have happened to *make* them gay. That simply wasn't the case.

This gave me the freedom to question and explore why people are gay. The more I talked with gay people and listened to their experiences, the more I realized that Lady Gaga was right: I was BORN THIS WAY!!!

Try to look at it this way: if the world was turned upside down and things were reversed and being gay was the norm and being heterosexual was the anomaly–would you be able to force yourself to love and be attracted to your same sex? What would it take for you to be able to physically do that? My guess is your answer is no. You were born THAT way. Nothing made you BE that way. You just are. And so it does for people in the LGBTQIA+ community.

14

Does this mean you are attracted to me (says the troll)?

Thankfully, I did not have many friends who questioned that when I came out to them. The funny thing is, the ones who did–were *not* attractive (sorry if you are reading this–I still love you, and I am sure someone is attracted to you, I just wasn't). I did NOT respond that way. I simply said, "are you attracted to *every* girl that you know?" To which they would always respond with a resounding "no."

Being gay is just like being straight–only the attraction is different. It doesn't make me not human. Gay people make fun of other gay people (though I wish we wouldn't because–kindness). Gay people are attracted to different kinds of gay people. Not every single gay person loves Ru Paul or Lady Gaga (though I don't understand why–they are both amazing). We don't all know Neil Patrick Harris (but I bet most of us want to). We use the same money as you (we don't use Euros–unless we are in Europe) even though it sounds like the best gay currency. We don't all do Pony Shows–though I would do a mean pony.

Anyway–all of that to say, you will KNOW* if I find you attractive! But don't assume that I am attracted to you just because you are a dude.

*you probably actually won't because I get wildly uncomfortable hitting on someone unless I know that they are already attracted to me. #SingleAndReadyToGetAwkwardAroundMenWhoAreAttractiveToMe

15

Why aren't you more feminine?

G irl, what you askin' that question to me for? Just kidding. I don't really say that. Unless you are a girl and have told me your pronouns and asked me that question.

Some people were very surprised when I came out. Others were not. I guess it depends on your perspective and how much you were around me.

If you met me on the street, I am pretty sure I am masculine presenting enough that you wouldn't assume I was gay–unless you got me to laugh–the giggle gives me away–every time (though apparently not in Utah where I grew up).

People often assumed I was straight or married with kids. Customers I would help at work would ALWAYS ask me about sports teams. I knew enough to pretend my way through. I would also frequently hear people say, "I don't want to keep you from your wife and kids, so I will make this quick (and then it was never quick, but that isn't the point). I simply had a good job, and I was/am relatively attractive–so why *wouldn't* I be married? Because I am gay, that's why!

I DO have a good personality, though. It really is where I shine.

I have loved seeing hyper masculine athletes coming out of the closet. I also love seeing celebrities that people absolutely thought were straight come out and live their truth. It isn't to rub it in anyone's face. It simply is for people to feel seen and represented.

The point is that not all gay people are flamboyant and effeminate. Just like all straight dudes aren't hyper-masculine and straight women aren't all "girly." No one has to be a certain way to be something.

16

Why can't you just fit in? (that's what HE said!)

There is a time and place where I DID fit in. I did what it took to stay safe. That doesn't mean that is what I should have done.

Have you ever been to a party where you didn't know anyone or where you felt completely out of place? If so, how did it make you feel? Have you ever been to a different church than you were raised in? How did it make you feel? Did you feel right at home, or were there customs uncomfortable to you?

I get that people can force themselves through some pretty uncomfortable and difficult situations, but why should they have to do that?

If you invited someone into your home and they didn't vibe with you, or you didn't vibe with them, why would you make them stay?

We all have the right to feel comfortable. We all have the right to be ourselves. The more we conform to the norms of society, the less we create. The less joy we experience. I said it earlier, but I will say it again–variety is the spice of life.

I would no more want to make you completely change your way of life to fit my standards and beliefs than I would want you to do the same to me.

Not fitting in is the new cool thing to do.

17

Why did you steal the rainbow?

F irst of all–we didn't *steal* it. We just use it. Anyone is welcome to use the rainbow–it is very inclusive–just like our community. It has different meanings for different people.

There are specific reasons that the rainbow is used to represent the LGBTQIA+ community. If you are feeling like you can't wear rainbow things because you are worried people will think you are gay–that just means we have progress to make. That is why the rainbow flag continues to evolve. The original one had each color representing something important to our community: see below*

Hot pink=*Sex*
Red=*Life*
Orange=*Healing*
Yellow=*Sunlight*
Green=*Nature*
Turquoise=*Magic*
Indigo=*Serenity*
Violet=*Spirit*

I like to think of it in my own way. To me, when people talk about God or things of a spiritual nature, there always seems to be some sort of discussion around a brilliant white light. People associate white with something being clean. A rainbow is refracted light. When broken down, a white light is really made up of all of these beautiful colors. I like to think that each diverse human coming together is what creates that beautiful white light. It takes ALL colors/kinds to be able to make what we associate with Godly things. I like to think that my color is either blue or red because they are my favorite colors. Everyone likes a different color for one reason or another, but maybe that is "their color" that makes them part of the greater collective of what makes us all beautiful in our own right and more beautiful when we come together to appreciate each color.

I wear rainbow things and have rainbow tattoos because even though I am "straight passing," I want others to see that there are people out there like them. I want a young gay man or woman to see my rainbows and not feel alone. I want them to feel seen and represented (even if I am not a full representation of who they are).

I have loved seeing athletes coming out of the closet. I have loved seeing celebrities that people absolutely thought were straight come out and live their truth. It isn't to rub it in anyone's face. It simply is for people to feel seen and represented.

Humans are funny that way—we feel less alone when we feel represented. That is why SO many Mormons wear CTR rings or BYU shirts and hats. They want other Mormons who see them—to know that they aren't alone. Sports lovers wear their favorite team jerseys, or shirts, or hats—because it connects them to other fans. It helps them bond and share their love of the game or the team with a stranger. Christians wear crosses around their necks or, hang them from their rearview mirrors, or put stickers on the backs of their cars. Are they rubbing it in people's faces? Do we see it that way? Maybe some do, but I think most don't. They also want to feel included. They also want to feel seen.

I could come up with a plethora of examples for all of this. At the end of the day, all of these things represent PRIDE in something important to them. When people are marginalized or belong to a minority group, it is much more important for them to be seen and feel heard. I'm SO grateful for the rainbow and what it represents for me.

Wear your rainbows with pride. If someone asks you if you are gay, you can simply say "no" unless you are…then I would encourage you to come out, in your own time, whenever you are ready. And by "come out" I actually prefer the term "invite in." You can invite others into something that is personal to you. It feels more calm to me. But you do you!

If you are afraid someone will treat you differently for sporting a rainbow—welcome to our world, that shouldn't exist. Help us to make it better. Help us change it so no one feels afraid to wear and fly rainbows. Make the world a more inclusive and colorful place!!!

18

Jesus, Gays, Greece, and Rome

You know what is interesting about all of these things? They existed all at the same time, and Jesus never once condemned the gays. If you look back at history, homosexuality was *rampant* in Rome and Greece during the time of Christ and after. If the gays were really going to be the downfall of society, you would think that Jesus would have been condemning them left and right–but he didn't. And neither should you.

Homosexuality has existed for thousands of years. Somehow, people just became afraid of it and stopped allowing it.

It makes me think of a lover who's been scorned. I have no way to prove this, but my theory is that there was a gay priest (they exist now, so they must have existed a long time ago) or religious leader who was in love with another man, but that it was an unrequited love. So, if that leader couldn't have the man he wanted, then NO MAN could. So he made up rules about not being able to be with another man which spawned from that.

But for real, I just don't think being gay is a real sin. Love is not a sin. Kindness and respect are not sins. We all play a part in this beautiful and crazy world. If you don't understand someone else's part or the role they play and that other person's part is not hurting anyone else—stay in your lane. Let them be happy. Let yourself be happy.

If you have any questions that I didn't answer and you wish I would have, feel free to give me a follow on Instagram and DM me. My handle is josephtanner16. I would be happy to answer any questions. If you read through this and are going to be mean in your comments, then you missed the point, and I will use my right to block you. :)

Thank you for purchasing my book. I would GREATLY appreciate it if you would give it a 5 star review on Amazon. I know you want to. It's pretty great. Much love and blessings to you and your life and your journey.

THE END
(or maybe just the beginning)

About the Author

Hi! I'm Joe. I'm an gay ex-Mormon living in the Boise area. I am the 3rd of 7 children, and am the uncle to 22 nieces and nephews. My passions are family, photography, movies, puzzles, books, and Taylor Swift. I am a self help book junkie and am obsessed with the work of Brene Brown and Adam Grant.